#HOLYMISCHIEF ADVENT CHALLENGE

REV DR SHANNON E KARAFANDA

For my family. Each of you bring me hope, love, joy, and peace. And a good bit of mischief too!

1 COME TO THE BEGINNING

Advent: To Come To

The word "Advent" is a Latin word meaning "to come to." We celebrate it in mainline denominations each year on the four Sundays leading up to Christmas. In one sense it is a time of preparation. To prepare our hearts for the savior born in humble beginnings and to prepare us for the second coming of this savior who will save us from this earth once again. Our God is transcendent so the preparation for what has happened and what will happen is the same in a very basic sense.

ADVENT IS A BEGINNING.

In another sense Advent is a beginning. There is no more waiting. Our King is here. We rejoice that God is with us.

. . .

THIS BRINGS us to another perception of Advent, the sense of wonder. Who are we that God Himself puts skin on and lives among us? What kind of love is this that He endures all that we endure? Why would He choose to do that?

THIS YEAR we need Advent like never before. Our world seems to be in a perpetual Lent - a time of somber reflection. Advent will allow us to turn that reflection into a time of preparation for the beginning of something new and the hope for what is to come. It will allow us to truly wonder once again who is God and that He want to be "with us"? Who is the Emmanuel?

FROM DECEMBER 1 - 25, read and focus on words that speak to your soul. Each word has a Biblical connection and can help us live into the season of Advent. The words would make a good focus for Centering Prayer each day but they can also help us get into some Holy Mischief.

WHAT IS HOLY MISCHIEF? I like to think of Holy Mischief as the mysterious disruption of the world with love.

WHAT THAT LOOKS like can be different for different people.

. . .

IT MIGHT MEAN WRITING an inspirational note for someone;

FOR ANOTHER PERSON it might mean giving their neighbor a gift anonymously.

FOR SOMEONE else it could mean praying for their enemies.

WE LIVE in a world that has a lot of negativity and our world really needs to experience something positive.

I BELIEVE that our faith proves that there truly can be more positive than negative in the world

THE GOSPEL MESSAGE is good news and Holy Mischief is one way to let that message break through the noise of the world.

YOUR ADVENT CHALLENGE IS THIS:
Purchase one item each day for your local food bank and write a word of encouragement on each one. You can use one of my words or some of your own. You can write a lot or a little. However you choose to live out this challenge

know that you are not only feeding someone physically, you are also feeding them spiritually.

MY LIST of words is below. Let Advent begin!

1. Joy
2. Peace
3. Kindness
4. Love
5. Hope
6. Wonder
7. Compassion
8. Happiness
9. Generosity
10. Abundance
11. Growth
12. Presence
13. Prayer
14. Life
15. Family
16. Worship
17. Rejoice
18. Health
19. Salvation
20. Light
21. Wisdom
22. Prepare
23. Return

2 JOY

Joy is an inward happiness that overflows and expresses itself outwardly. Joy is usually caused by something exceptionally good or satisfying.

WE OFTEN TALK about the joy at Christmas time.
>   Jesus was exceptionally good.
>   His birth was the exception to the idea of a messiah.
>   He came as a baby.
>   Presented first to the shepherds.
>   One of the lowest professions.

BUT THE JOY comes not only from the circumstances of his birth but by the meaning of his presence in the world.

GOD IS WITH US.
>   Emmanuel.

. . .

WHEN OUR JOY comes from being close to the presence of God, our joy is eternal. Christmas joy is more than exceptionally good. It is transformational.

> *"And the angel said unto them, Fear not: for, behold, I bring you good tidings of great joy, which shall be to all people. For unto you is born this day in the city of David a Savior, which is Christ the Lord."*
> *Luke 2:10-11 KJV*

3 PEACE

Peace doesn't happen when everything is right. Peace happens when we are aware of many options and choose what is right.

Peace isn't a result of circumstances. It is a state of mind and a state of being made possible by the Holy Spirit.

When we think of peace, we often think of a sense of calm and tranquility. However, true peace is something that is cultivated in the midst of chaos. It is not a lack of feeling or an absence of emotion. Peace is the ability to be present in the midst of turmoil and to still have a clear mind and an open heart.

It can be difficult to find peace in the world today. There is so much noise and distraction. We are constantly bombarded with images and messages that tell us we are not good enough and that we need more. We are constantly comparing ourselves to others and trying to live up to unrealistic standards.

However, if we learn to look for peace within ourselves, we can find it everywhere. It is in the moments of stillness and quiet that we connect with our innermost selves. It is in the moments when we are kind and compassionate even when we don't feel like it. It is in the moments when we choose love over hate, even when it is difficult.

Peace is something that we have to work for. It doesn't come easy and it doesn't come automatically. But it is worth the effort. When we find peace within ourselves, we find compassion, kindness, love, and joy. We find hope for the future and a sense of calm. We find God's presence in our lives.

The world may be erupting in chaos. Our souls may feel that chaos around us. Choosing peace isn't ignoring those disruptions but accepting that those disruptions are a part of life and that with God there is a way through them.

> *"And the peace of God, which passeth all*
> *understanding, shall keep your hearts*
> *and minds through Christ Jesus."*
> *Philippians 4:7 KJV*

4 KINDNESS

The root of the word kindness means "noble deeds," "nation," or "to produce an increase." It seems like kindness cannot be done in a bubble. Thinking kind thoughts, while positive, is not the same as being kind. Our kindness connects us and increases our faith through our witness to the Holy Spirit.

KINDNESS IS one of the most important traits we can possess. It is the quality that allows us to see the best in others, even when they don't see it themselves. Kindness is the quality that allows us to forgive, even when we have been hurt deeply. And kindness is the quality that allows us to give of ourselves, even when we don't have much to give.

KINDNESS IS NOT EASY. It often requires us to put our own feelings and desires aside and to think about others. It often means doing something that we don't want to do or that is difficult. But it is always worth it.

WHEN WE ARE KIND, we connect with others in a deep and meaningful way. We show them that they are valued and loved. We show them that there is hope for the future. We show them that there is light in the darkness.

KINDNESS IS a sign of love and compassion. It is a sign of hope and peace. It is a sign of God's presence in our lives.

> *"But the fruit of the Spirit is love, joy, peace, forbearance, kindness, goodness, faithfulness,"*
> *Galatians* 5:22 *NIV*

5 LOVE

There is nothing greater.

Christmas is a time when we are reminded of the love that God has for us. It is a time when we celebrate the birth of Jesus Christ, and it is a time when we remember His sacrifice for our sins. It is also a time when we are reminded of the importance of love. Love is at the heart of the Christmas story, and it is at the heart of our salvation. Without love, we would be lost. But because of love, we can be saved. Christmas is a time to celebrate that love. It is a time to celebrate the birth of our Savior, and it is a time to remember His sacrifice for us. And it is also a time to remind ourselves of the importance of love in our own lives. Love is what makes Christmas special. It is what makes our salvation possible. And it is what will ultimately make our lives complete. So let us all remember the true meaning of Christmas this year: love. Love for God, love for one another, and love for ourselves.

"For God so loved the world that he gave his one and only Son, that whoever believes in him shall not perish but have eternal life. For God did not send his Son into the world to condemn the world, but to save the world through him."

John 3:16-17 NIV

6 HOPE

There's a difference between hope and wishes.

WISHES AREN'T dependent on me. They are dependent on luck. Or an external force that has no investment in the person or situation.

HOPE REQUIRES INVESTMENT BY SOMEONE. It is a belief that when I've done all I can, God will fill in the gaps.

IT'S a meeting of heaven and earth.

HOPE IS INCARNATIONAL.

"And hope does not put us to shame,
because God's love has been poured out
into our hearts through the Holy Spirit,
who has been given to us."
Romans 5:5 NIV

7 WONDER

Wonder causes an intelligent person to question what they know. And to live in that uncertainty.

IN TODAY'S SOCIETY, we are constantly told to "know" things. We are bombarded with facts and figures, statistics and data. And as a result, we often lose sight of the beauty of ignorance. We forget that not knowing can be just as wonderful as knowing. We forget to wonder.

WONDER IS the ability to see the world through fresh eyes. It is the ability to look at something familiar and see it for the first time. It is the ability to approach life with curiosity and openness, without judgment or preconceived notions. Wonder is what allows us to experience true amazement and astonishment in the world around us. It is what makes life a journey of discovery, instead of a mundane procession from one day to the next.

WONDER IS a precious commodity in today's world. It is something that we all too often take for granted. But it is something that we should never take for granted, because it is what makes life worth living. So let us all remember to appreciate the wonders of this world, and let us all remember to wonder at the beauty of life itself.

> *"Therefore once more I will astound these people with wonder upon wonder; the wisdom of the wise will perish, the intelligence of the intelligent will vanish.""*
> *Isaiah 29:14 NIV*

8 HAPPINESS

Barak

The Hebrew word for bless is barak which means "to kneel" or "to show respect." The Greek word for blessed is makarios which means "happy" or "blissful." In both cases happiness or blessedness does not happen in a vacuum. Happiness happens when we are in relationship with God or with other people. When we worship or show respect, then we are happy. Not due to circumstances but due to the source of our happiness in God.

> *"Happy are the people to whom such bless-*
> *ings fall; happy are the people whose*
> *God is the Lord."*
> *Psalms 144:15 NRSV*

9 GENEROSITY

One of the marks of a truly generous person is that they are always ready to help, even when they themselves are in need. This was certainly true of C.S. Lewis, who was always willing to give of his time and talents, even when he was struggling with health issues or grieving the loss of a loved one. Lewis once said that it is not how much we give that matters, but how much love we put into our giving. And his own life was a testimony to this truth. Lewis was a man of deep faith, and he believed that it was our duty to help those in need. He once wrote, "There is no solace like love. And in giving it away, we experience our own deepest happiness." Lewis's words challenge us to think about how we can be more generous in our own lives.

THERE IS a proverb that talks about "a generous person." A better translation from Hebrew is "a person of blessing." Generosity is more than giving.

. . .

IT IS GIVING with a heart like God's.
> It is giving to enrich someone's life.
> It is giving that is often unearned and unmerited.
> It is giving that transforms the world.
> It is love.

AND WHEN WE are generous like that, the act of giving blesses and transforms us too.

> *"A generous person will be enriched, and*
> *one who gives water will get water."*
> *Proverbs 11:25 NRSV*

10 ABUNDANCE

Abundance isn't always a good thing.

You can have an abundance of termites that can destroy your home. You can have an abundance of caution that might offer safety but might keep you from an opportunity. You can have an abundance of chocolate that is great if you space out your consumption but horrible if you eat it all at once. You can have an abundance of money that divides your family or is squandered by bad habits.

OR YOU CAN HAVE an abundance of life. That doesn't mean you'll live longer. It isn't talking about time or eternal life. This is abundant life. A life worth living. A life where love overflows. A life walking with God and knowing He's always with you.

"The thief comes only to steal and kill and destroy. I came that they may have life, and have it abundantly."
John 10:10 NRSV

11 GROWTH

How can we grow spiritually? It is a lifelong process that begins with an openness to God and a willingness to grow. Just as a plant needs sunlight and water to grow, we need God's grace and love to help us grow spiritually. The first step is to develop a relationship with God through prayer and worship. As we get to know God better, we begin to realize His will for our lives and our need for Him. We also start to see the areas of our lives where we need to grow. We must carefully tend to ourselves in order to thrive, and so must our faith be nurtured through regular study of the Bible, meditation, service, and fellowship with other believers. As we allow God to work in our lives, we will slowly but surely begin to see growth in our faith.

GROWTH IS NOT something we do. It is something that happens.

We can nurture it.

We can tend to it.

We can guard it.

BUT WE CAN'T MAKE it happen. Only God can. Our job is to make sure conditions are at their best. And if we are lucky we get to watch the blooming happen.

> *"I planted, Apollos watered, but God gave the growth."*
> 1 *Corinthians* 3:6 *NRSV*

12 PRESENCE

Being present is more of a gift than you know. When you are present with someone physically, you start to resonate with that person. Your body chemistry responds to their voice, smell, and appearance. When you are mentally present with someone, telling stories and sharing moments, your brain waves start to synchronize.

GOD IS PRESENT WITH US. Emmanuel means "God with us." God changes who we are when we accept that He is there and we are in turn present with Him.

HOW COULD it be that the omnipotent, all-knowing, and good God is present to us sinners? In scripture, we are told that "God is love" (1 John 4:8). And what is love but self-giving? To say that "God is present to us" means that He gives Himself to us. He willingly comes down from heaven and becomes one of us. He deals with us as a friend, as a brother, and as a father. And not only does He come down to our level, but He goes even lower. He doesn't stop at becoming a man; He becomes a servant. A criminal. A corpse. All for our sake. This is the sort of God we have. The all-powerful, all-knowing, and good God is present to us not in judgments and wrath, but in mercy and love! Thanks be to God!

> *"Tremble, O earth, at the presence of the Lord, at the presence of the God of Jacob,"*
> *Psalms 114:7 NRSV*

13 PRAYER

God,

Scripture says you hear our prayers so here goes: We are messed up. We know we need to love others but we look for faults. We criticize. We pick sides and in doing so vilify the other side. We are overwhelmed by the divisiveness, the sickness, the hurt, the pain. And we just..can't..anymore.

We are sorry.

Fix us. Overwhelm us with your love. Heal those who are hurting physically, emotionally, mentally, and spiritually so that we may be healed.

By the power of your Holy Spirit, make this world new once more. Help us to break down the barriers we have built up to guard our hearts against feeling anything so that we can once again feel your powerful presence working in us, making this world a better place.

We love you.

Amen.

"Therefore confess your sins to one another, and pray for one another, so that you may be healed. The prayer of the righteous is powerful and effective."
James 5:16 NRSV

14 LIFE

Living the life that Jesus promised doesn't mean our life is perfect. It means God walks with us through it.

A LIFE of faith is not a life spent waiting for things to happen. It is not a life spent waiting for answers to come. It is a life lived in confident trust that God knows what He is doing, even when we do not. It is a life lived in hope, even when all around us seems dark and hopeless. It is a life lived in love, even when those around us are unlovable. A life of faith is not easy. It takes courage to step out into the unknown, trusting that God will be there with us. But it is worth it, for through faith we find strength, hope, and joy that the world cannot give. So let us not be afraid to live a life of faith, confident in the knowledge that God holds us in His hands.

. . .

GOD ILLUMINATES the path as we go. Holds us steady when we stumble. Never leaves us when we fall but will sit with us when we aren't ready to get back up. And when we are walking or running down the path, God expects us to offer that same light and stability to others.

> "in him was life, and the life was the light of
>   all people."
> John 1:4 NRSV

15 FAMILY

Family isn't who you are related to. Family is who you relate to. When we begin to see everyone as family and treat everyone like family, no one gets left behind.

THE FAMILY of God is made up of everyone who relates to Him. When we begin to see everyone as family and treat everyone like family, no one gets left behind. Because God is love, He willingly comes down from heaven and becomes one of us, dealing with us as a friend, brother, and father. And not only does He come down to our level, but He goes even lower.

> "But Ruth said, "Do not press me to leave
> you or to turn back from following you!
> Where you go, I will go; where you
> lodge, I will lodge; your people shall be
> my people, and your God my God."

Ruth 1:16 NRSV

16 WORSHIP

Worship isn't an event on the calendar, taking place on a certain day at a certain place. Worship is a way of living. It is intentionally being present with God and showing God adoration and love in ways that we show to no one else.

WORSHIP IS LIVING a life of gratitude and thanksgiving, letting go of our own desires to align with God's will. It is giving our all, body and soul, to Him as an offering of worship. It is a constant offering throughout our entire lives.

LIVE your life in grateful alignment with God. When you worship Him in this way, it becomes easier to let go of your own desires and give Him your all. Let us not forget the importance of worship in our lives, but rather make it a daily habit that brings us into His presence with gladness.

*"Worship the Lord with gladness; come into
his presence with singing."*
Psalms 100:2 NRSV

17   REJOICE

There are a lot of things that bring me joy:

- holidays with my family,
- singing Hamilton songs in the car,
- puppies,
- kittens,
- bacon,
- Christmas lights,
- the first cup of coffee in the morning,
- a long walk on the beach,
- bacon,
- my boys coming home to visit from college,
- watching my daughter play basketball or soccer,
- date night,
- laughing so hard and not being able to stop,
- bacon.

BUT WHEN I REJOICE, I don't just feel joy; I experience it. Not only do I feel great joy, but I also reflect that joy back to its source. Rejoicing in God is the reciprocity of joy without the expectation of reciprocity. And it doesn't just happen when we worship or pray or read the Bible.

IT CAN HAPPEN...ALWAYS.

> *"Rejoice in the Lord always; again I will say, Rejoice."*
> *Philippians 4:4 NRSV*

18 HEALTH

It is well...

Health, wholeness, and salvation are intimately connected. We tend to compartmentalize so many different aspects of our lives including our health. But our health is intricately connected to our spiritual health. In the simplest of ways, if we don't feel well, we won't have the energy or mindset to nurture our faith. Just as we need to exercise our bodies to stay physically fit, we need to exercise our faith muscles to stay spiritually fit.

ONE WAY TO think of health as a spiritual discipline is to consider the analogy of physical fitness. When we work out, we are putting stress on our bodies. But if we don't put stress on our bodies, they will atrophy and become weak. In the same way, when we face trials and difficult situations, we are putting stress on our faith muscles. But if we never face any challenges, our faith will become weak and timid.

So instead of avoiding challenges, we should see them as opportunities to grow in faith.

OUR RELATIONSHIP with God needs to be nurtured if it is going to grow. We need to spend time in prayer and Bible reading, and we need to be involved in a community of believers where we can worship God together.

ONE THING IS FOR SURE: if we want to have a strong relationship with God, we need to take care of our physical health just as much as our spiritual health.

TAKE care of your health so that you can be all God called and created you to be.

> *"Beloved, I pray that all may go well with*
> *you and that you may be in good health,*
> *just as it is well with your soul."*
> 3 John 1:2 NRSV

19 SALVATION

Salvation is a gift.

An unearned gift resulting from our faith.

It isn't a ticket to a destination.

It is deliverance from our current one into a better way of living.

Salvation doesn't make our lives easier. It makes them complete.

Salvation makes us one with Jesus now. Not in the future but now.

EMMANUEL.

God with us.

The best gift ever.

> "For by grace you have been saved through
> faith, and this is not your own doing; it
> is the gift of God—"

Ephesians 2:8 *NRSV*

20 LIGHT

In early theories of optics (the study of light), vision fell into two camps:

1. Vision originates in the object we see.
2. Vision originates in our eyes.

IN REALITY the vision we experience happens in a triune relationship between the object, our eyes, and light. Leave any one of these out and we are blind.

SPIRITUAL BLINDNESS HAPPENS in a similar triune relationship. We see the world. The world sees us. God sees the world. God sees us. When we begin to see ourselves and the world the way God sees both, our eyes are open we are no longer blind but the light of God allows us to see.

> *"Your word is a lamp to my feet and a light*
> *to my path."*
> *Psalms 119:105 NRSV*

21 WISDOM

I used to think wisdom was all about gaining knowledge.
    So I read a lot.
    And studied a lot.
    And learned a lot.

BUT I WASN'T any wiser.

SO I TOOK a step in faith.
    And I asked God to give me wisdom.
    And He gave me a task: LOVE

THE MORE I DO, the wiser I become.
    Knowledge is wasted if you never use it.
    Go and love.

> *"If any of you is lacking in wisdom, ask*
> *God, who gives to all generously and*
> *ungrudgingly, and it will be given you."*
> *James 1:5 NRSV*

22 PREPARE

When we thinking about preparing a way for someone, we often think exclusively of clearing the path. Getting rid of debris. Making sure there are no dangers in the road ahead.

BUT PREPARATION ISN'T JUST about clearing the path. It is also about making the path one that is worthy of traveling on. Who will we meet along the path? Are there people cheering the way? Is the path beautiful, reflecting the glory of the creation of God?

DURING ADVENT we think about spiritually preparing for Christ's return. We ask for forgiveness and we wait in the stillness. But there's another aspect: preparing for joy.

SOMETIMES THE DECORATIONS of Christmas get criticized as adding to the cultural, commercial aspect of

Christmas. But if it brings you joy, build them up. Let everything that you do prepare the way for God.

> *"It shall be said, "Build up, build up,*
> *prepare the way, remove every obstruc-*
> *tion from my people's way.""*
> *Isaiah 57:14 NRSV*

23 RETURN

I love companies that have very generous return policies - stores that take back an item that has been well used or is past the time of the return policy. I tend to shop again at those stores, knowing that they really want me to enjoy their products. They don't get irritated that I'm back in their store trying to get my money back. They are just happy that I'm there.

RETURN POLICIES CAN MAKE or break a company. A generous one says a lot about the value they place on their creations. When we create something, it is ours and we want others to value it the way we do.

IT TAKES a bit of effort to return something. It isn't always easy even with a liberal policy. But it's worth it.

. . .

YOU KNOW IT'S TRUE. And you can also see the metaphor underneath.

> *"What shall I return to the Lord for all his*
> *bounty to me?"*
> *Psalms 116:12 NRSV*

24 COMFORT

God doesn't call us to be comfortable. God calls us to take risks. Yet God doesn't ask us to take those risks without equipping us. Every step of the way God is present with us and will guide us to where we need to go.

IN THAT WAY, we can have comfort in God. But that doesn't mean we are comfortable. Comfort often means complacency and a false sense of security. God wants us to be secure in Him, but that doesn't mean we will always be comfortable.

EMBRACE the discomfort and risk of following God. And find comfort in knowing that you are never alone.

"Even though I walk through the darkest

> *valley, I fear no evil; for you are with me; your rod and your staff— they comfort me."*
> Psalms 23:4 NRSV

25 REMEMBER

When we get to Christmas, it's hard to forget where we are. We've been in preparation and the time is here.

WE REMEMBER past Christmases and the wonder of our childhood.

We remember more recent Christmases and the loved ones that we can't celebrate with anymore.

We remember all the things on our to do list that don't need to get done now.

We remember that we said we were going to scale back this year.

We remember how much we hate that one Christmas song or movie and can't wait for that part of the season to be over.

We remember to check on our neighbor.

We remember that today a light shines in the darkness and the darkness cannot overcome it.

We remember we are thankful. Thankful for our God. Thankful for our family. Thankful for this moment.

IT'S hard to forget today. May we always have signs to help us remember.

> *"I thank my God every time I remember*
>   *you,"*
> *Philippians 1:3 NRSV*

ABOUT THE AUTHOR

Rev Dr Shannon E Karafanda is a renegade Executive Pastor serving Peachtree City United Methodist Church. If you can spell her last name, you can find her bio online via any social media outlet but one common thread you'll see is that she's a professional ***#HolyMischief*** Maker.

Everyday she does one personal challenge to disrupt someone's day with love. And she leads an online community of over 1200 members who aspire to do the same. Her online community of #HolyMischief makers, challenges each other to love neighbors and strangers for no reason other than it's a bit scary and a lot of fun. Not to mention it transforms the world...starting with us.

If she's not online, you'll probably find her running, reading, binge watching Marvel shows, playing with her dog, planning her next adventure or drinking wine but not necessarily at the same time.

She did her doctoral research because of a book suggestion given over chips and salsa. It was life changing (both the book and the salsa). The book was Mindset and ever since then she's made it a goal to live into a growth mindset instead of a fixed mindset. The difference between our desires and achievements seem infinite at times. But our mindset can narrow the difference to one single step.

If you are ready to take the next step toward changing the world, let's go! For more, go to www.ShannonKarafanda.com.

ALSO BY REV DR SHANNON E KARAFANDA

The Synergy Shift

When the team at Lighthouse United Methodist Church got together to dream about what their new church would be like, they created synergy. But when Lead Pastor Allan Todd passed away suddenly, they were left with a void they weren't sure how to fill. That was until a new pastor, Mark Jordan, was appointed and the congregation was able to grieve and move on.

Shannon Karafanda (Lighthouse's Associate Pastor) tells this personal story of a church that learned some funny and touching lessons from two Lead Pastors when the synergy shifted from one to another.

#HolyMischief Lenten Challenge

Lent is a time of repentance, fasting, and preparation for the coming of Easter. The season of Lent often creates an opportunity to take up a spiritual discipline to draw closer to God. Sometimes it is fasting or journaling, and sometimes it is doing a daily devotional reading.

But what if your season of Lent was to combine the power of a spiritual discipline with doing an act of kindness and reflecting on how you experienced God's love in doing so. Rev Dr Shannon E Karafanda, a United Methodist Pastor, has carefully curated 40 different #HolyMischief challenges during Lent. Each one connects to scripture and allows you to embody a deeper sense of the Word. Come along on the journey and complete each challenge as we move towards Easter.